WRONG NUMBER

poems by

Katrin Talbot

Finishing Line Press
Georgetown, Kentucky

WRONG NUMBER

Publisher: Leah Huete de Maines

Editor: Christen Kincaid

Cover Art: Katrin Talbot

Author Photo: Ariana Karp

Cover Design: Katrin Talbot

Order online: www.finishinglinepress.com
also available on amazon.com

Author inquiries and mail orders:
Finishing Line Press
PO Box 1626
Georgetown, Kentucky 40324
USA

Table of Contents

If the Phone
Doesn't ring,
It's me.
—Jimmy Buffett

On August 4, 1922 at 6:30 p.m. EST, North Americans paid
tribute to Alexander Graham Bell by not using their telephones
for one minute during his funeral service.

Delivered By Mistake

Mistake was a skinny kid,
stressed and behind on
deliveries because
it was the day after Saturday night
it was Valentine's Day
it was snowy

Someone had
heard wrong
written wrong
typed wrong

The bouquet was the usual
fabulous clash of
seasons, of latitudes:
birds of paradise squawking above
Dutch tulips, with
westcoast hydrangeas
waiting for the ethylene's
signal to ripen

Mistake was all about
following orders—
military mom, preacher dad—
so the arrangement landed
at the wrong house,
placed in front of the
right painting,
reported and
now singing

Monomorium minimum

They showed up in the fall after
the horrific floodings
Wrong address, I told them,
as I might mop the floor daily,
Sugar Ants

They didn't believe me and
moved in

Nowadays, I give them sweet
boric acid to carry back to their
villas and the five-year-old
gives them
names

Caught in the Act

The fossil told the story—
the double death in
Green River, Wyoming
Mioplosus swallowing *Knightia*
It could be a testament to greed,
an ode to the childhood dinner mantra
Your eyes were bigger then your stomach
The perch snatched the herring
before fully assessing possibility,
feasibility, just plain ability

Hunger captured in
river tales, solidified,
the act of killing so *active*,
that frozen moment now
haunting, fascinating after
all these fifty million
years

Prank

Which line did *you* use as a kid
with your friend when you randomly dialed
and asked a question? Ours was
Is your refrigerator running?
Then go catch it!

She was the grandniece of
Walter Cronkite and
she had the confidence
of her great uncle on
the phone in the basement office,
while we nibbled on
the burned experiments
of her Home Ec teacher mother

My role, as I would have been
a disaster on the phone,
shackled by guilt and discomfort,
was the designated giggler, and
karma arrived with
soda flying out of
my nose

After all these behaving decades,
I still remember it,
the burn of soda,
discomfort's lasting
sting

Wrong Number

My son, who doesn't
exist, apparently was
involved in an
incident on the bus—
making pretty serious
threats to another boy
so is suspended from
riding the bus Monday
to his elementary school
somewhere in Wisconsin

I call back, of course,
still shaking from
a school call,
elementary school,
our children

One Off

Years ago, his number was
one off from Chicago's FBI tip line
He was Polish, a pianist,
always worried
about concerts,
memory slips and
old country authorities

This didn't help—all the calls
about impendings, leads,
secret after secret

And no-one would believe
his wrong number line—
his accent, his protests
So he heard the whispered stories,
some of them hammering
their stakes deep into
his sleep

Would *you* have hung up?

The Moment When You Drop in on Your Life

And wonder why
you are barreling along
an interstate,
which you can barely
see because the heavy rain is
almost obliterating
lane lines, shoulder stripes,
especially since you
are going 73 mph like
everybody else and
at eleven p.m., the visibility
is reduced

Too fast
And you realize your
mortality potential is
hanging on by a thread or two
as you anchor your sights
to the taillights ahead
and wish everyone would just
slow down,
but knowing we all want to get
off this black satin ribbon,
back into a safer nightmare

Control

The young couple
walked into the room
where I was typing poems to order

Some approached with effortless intention,
others lightly shackled by hesitation
The quiet young woman selected
three words from the basket and
the young man stood behind her but
told her to put CONTROL on top

I wanted to type
RUN!
and hand her the one word
love poem

Lemon Vs. January

The one from August
still hanging, ripening against
the non-Meyer season on
the other side of the glass,
the other side of winter,
in an inside orchard of one
in a room of sunshine

The way I try and fail,
my Australian wiring of
summers in December
still chanting silently against
the bitter cold of
my chosen,
my by-default
climate

Dialing In

The year he would
accidentally call her
number more
then his wife's
more than her husband's

Her son began
to notice
the concept of
speed dial,
the lightness of
apology,
the gilt of
her laughter

Losing

A game,
a love,
a friend

It is a carving into
of sorts,
the shape of
Had

And your only task now
is to examine,
cherish, and
release

Borders

It was a simple call to
Borders Books,
a search for a title
He answered and the word Borders,
historically a crisp declaration,
had never sounded so lovely,
soft British velvet

Have you ever fallen in love
with a voice?
I'm not talking about
radio personalities, opera,
or the low sexy German GPS
voice that a brother-in-law employed
to help him find his way until my sister
switched it to a practical abrupt male voice

I wanted to keep inquiries flowing,
chat about the subject, feel smarter, sharper
But I thanked him, and let him hang up
on the number I wanted him to have,
at that moment, as
Her

Back In the Day

The Old Guard resented the New Chair—
they couldn't get away with
what they were used to

This was a music department,
and power was a prominent ingredient in
the Department of Egos

So they began their war
middle school bullies, frat boys,
all grown up

The first night, they called many
pizza parlours—big city,
had them all deliver to his house

This was back in the days of
paying on delivery,
the doorbell scramble for wallet

With this incessant strategy,
the chipping away at confidence,
the chairman soon died of a
heart attack

How many pizzas are
too many pizzas?

Seventy-Six

It's enough for trombones,
for bicentennials,
for cruising along I90

Enough
So why is 97 mph necessary
when it's not about you,
but 97 percent about what
you do to others,
your driving family,
whose potential to
suffer deeply from your
weaving adrenaline levels
is frightening
as you fly by baby-on-boards,
someone's grampa,
a maid of honour on the way
to the wedding
And me, who could be you,
but choose
not to be?

History Lesson

My first cell phone held
the previous number of
a Wisconsin Party Boy
So many messages about
spontaneous hangs—
was he a recreational drug dealer or
the guy who always showed up
with a sixpack?
His mother called once and I asked her to
please make a note,
tell his friends about
his seven new numbers
She ended up calling several more times,
as did his buddies

I wondered—should I start sobbing
and inform them
he was no longer with us *or*
tell them his phone privileges had been
taken away for a week?
I had all the power now in
this land of Wrong

Cello as Don Juan

Back in the day,
they were stewardesses
Back in the day,
he could usually slip his
cello into the garment bag closet
If not, the cello got the coveted
bulkhead window, FAA regulations

After awhile, he'd ask on boarding
for a seat-belt extender and
do it himself to avoid
the predictable fussing and bosom-
heaving trying to secure the cello
He was tired of the predictable slip
of their phone numbers,
feeling like a piece of cello meat

Even when he got that big gold
wedding band—on his right hand
because of the lefthand playing—
in America, he was still
unmarried in their eyes
They loved giving him two meals because
he had paid for a cello ticket,
they loved the imagined dazzle
of a performer, a soloist,
the formal attire,
the ovations

They still slipped him their
number, even when he
boarded with his wife,
because she rarely got to

sit with him,
up at the front with his
other wife, the ancient
wooden one

BadAss

My daughter threw that cloak
over my shoulders, not me,
but after the deed was done,
I did feel a deep resonance
in the adrenaline stampede,
the one that happened
after I grabbed
that juvenile by
its possum tail,
pulled it out of
the chicken coop and
threw it like a squealing horseshoe,
like a muttering discus,
into the far snowbank
to put an end to the discussion
about the possibility of
sharing a coop with
my darlings

Time Signature

Something backed into my
dreams, early morning,
on the other side of
waking wall

I was counting the beats,
seeing, assessing if it
was in 5/4 or ¾,
worried about a Stravinsky score
I hadn't studied enough
and once I stumbled through
Awake's taut membrane,
I realized it wasn't Igor,
just BackUp Chevy who is
always in 4/4

I made coffee and settled
down to some score study,
to fend off some of
the nocturnal
scolding

Seventy-Nine

As chair, she decided that
He's too old
The faculty had requested him
as guest artist—
first violinist of
the Guarneri Quartet,
chamber music god,
author, storyteller, mensch

They begged. For the students.
No—he's Too Old

A closet full of
parental issues
that go bump in
her nights

A Situation in 23A

I heard someone crying
a few rows ahead
or behind—
unclear from the plane's
tubal acoustic,
as we prepared
for take off

A breakup,
a grandmother,
an unbearable transition

What could I do?
How could I help, fix, stop,
interfere…

What right had I to
double-park my life
next to hers
and assume I could, should,
comfort

So I sat and stared out
my window, watching life
rush under the wings,
feeling, without fighting it,
the unendurables we
carry around,
and eventually try to,
need to acquit and
release

Quantification of Poultry

Flock of four older
plus two new very younger
equals six

Add fear, minus two
over the fence
equals four
plus one hundred aches

Return to safety
of one little one, the other one
back the next morning

What does one plus
one long night in
the world of predators equal?

Percentages

Where would Dante have placed
the *divine wind* Kamakaze pilots,
the original suicide bombers?

Death vs. defeat
paying their debt,
showing their love for
family and emperor,
the Emperor who would only
indignantly notice that
they were part of the 87%
honouring him
whose attacks didn't
meet the circled mark

Moscow, 1982

The Eastern Bloc cellists had been given
seven months to prepare for
the famed Tchaikovsky Competition,
the Western cellists, two months
He was, he was told,
high up on the totem pole

All through the night
before performances,
the phone would ring on the hour,
a held silence on the other end

Until he unplugged the phone

But they could still
knock and
disappear

Knock and
disappear

One way or another,
they had his
number

Two Seconds as an Angel

They rang the bell
and declared their mission today—
to focus on wholesome music
for the family values movement
in their church's broader society

I told them we were both
classical musicians and
apparently a halo appeared over
my questionable angelic head
but one of them grabbed it
immediately and claimed it as
her own, so I really had
only two seconds as an angel

Because of that, I wanted to reveal
all my sins there in the doorway,
dirty up the pristine waters that
the pamphlet women were floating on

But I smiled, took their literature
for future reference or
a poem and
closed the door against
the unpleasant whiff of
self-righteous

Decades ago,
before caller ID
and answering machines,
we'd have to pick up
most calls
because it could be
bad news
heart-stopping news
howling news
or
good news
or
beige news
but mostly because it could be
bad news

One evening I picked up
—a fellow selling cable—
I told him we don't watch
television much

He seemed enraged
MAY I ASK WHY NOT?!!
as though the FBI was
onto us and our Anti-American activity

I took a breath,
back before taking a breath
was mandated,
and told him
we were just really busy people
and he, thankfully,
hung up on me

Lower Math

He got on the wrong bus—
new to the city, easy to do,
met her, married,
moved to the burbs,
wrong house in the right
neighbourhood—
leaky pipes, loose hinges,
and soon,
screaming triplets
Two plus three equaled
twenty-three

But one night they did the math,
the stressed math,
the tired math,
the love math
and calculated it equaled one
and that pretty much
summed it up

Numbered

The days until spring
the hours to deadlines
Subtract or add
one in the manner of
an organized worrier,
an organized warrior

Three by three,
the way she counts her
knitting casts,
two by two,
the kindergarten outing,
two by four, the chicken coop build,
one by one
days 'til the wedding
'til a graduation
'til the moment of
a reverse numbering,
the final days, numbered

The tune was wrong
when I dialed you
Dialed you in 7/4,
but the tonal row
had a leap of fourth
I didn't know

I didn't know you'd
pick up anyway and
pretend you were
an old farmer
stuck in the burbs
but we ended up
having a lovely conversation,
didn't we, especially about piglets,
before the final apology,
the final tone

Nomenclature

It is known that,
or believed that
Hershey's Kisses
are appropriately
named
until you
have actually been
kissed

Counting

The clouds
for an hour,
with the numbers
changing and
sometimes turning into
three, four,
buckle my shoe,
but what does it matter
when rhyme is an
occasional concept
in the wild prairie of
language, when you are
under two and the world is
bigger and so much
smaller than the
sky you gaze up at
fading blue punctuated
with cloud rabbits as
you lie next to nana in
the clover and talk
about birdies,
mosquitoes, and
a tickle

What did you expect when you gave your phone to the monkey?

Australian-born **Katrin Talbot**'s collection *The Waiting Room for the Imperfect Alibis* was just released from Kelsay Books and *The Devil Orders A Latte* and *Falling Asleep at the Circus* are forthcoming from Fernwood Press and Turning Point Books respectively. She has been a finalist for the Yellowwood Poetry Prize, Artsmith Literary Contest, the Bridge Poetry Prize and Phoebe's Greg Grummer Prize and has six other chapbooks, two Pushcart Prize nominations and quite a few chickens. She also makes noise on the viola in the Madison Symphony Orchestra. www.katrintalbot.com

www.ingramcontent.com/pod-product-compliance
Lightning Source LLC
Chambersburg PA
CBHW022049080426
42734CB00009B/1285